school - 学校	2
travel - 旅行	5
transport - 交通运输	8
city - 城市	10
landscape - 地形	14
restaurant - 餐馆	17
supermarket - 超市	20
drinks - 饮料	22
food - 食物	23
farm - 农场	27
house - 房子	31
living room - 客厅	33
kitchen - 厨房	35
bathroom - 浴室	38
child's room - 儿童房	42
clothing - 衣服	44
office - 办公室	49
economy - 经济	51
occupations - 职业	53
tools - 工具	56
musical instruments - 乐器	57
zoo - 动物园	59
sports - 体育	62
activities - 活动	63
family - 家	67
body - 身体	68
hospital - 医院	72
emergency - 紧急情况	76
Earth - 地球	77
clock - 钟表	79
week - 周	80
year - 年	81
shapes - 形状	83
colours - 颜色	84
opposites - 反义词	85
numbers - 数字	88
languages - 语言	90
who / what / how - 谁/什么/怎样	91
where - 方位	92

Impressum
Verlag: BABADADA GmbH, Nedderfeld 112 , 22529 Hamburg
Geschäftsführer / Verlagsleitung: Harald Hof
Druck: Books on Demand GmbH, In de Tarpen 42, 22848 Norderstedt

Imprint
Publisher: BABADADA GmbH, Nedderfeld 112 , 22529 Hamburg, Germany
Managing Director / Publishing direction: Harald Hof
Print: Books on Demand GmbH, In de Tarpen 42, 22848 Norderstedt

classroom
教室

divide
除

186/2

board
黑板

school yard
校园

teacher
老师

write
书写

paper
纸

pen
钢笔

desk
办公桌

ruler
直尺

book
书

pupil
学生

satchel
书包

pencil case
铅笔盒

pencil
铅笔

pencil sharpener
卷笔刀

rubber
橡皮擦

drawing pad
画板

drawing

图画

paintbrush

画笔

paint box

颜料盒

scissors

剪刀

glue

胶水

exercise book

练习册

homework

家庭作业

number

数字

add

加

subtract

减

multiply

乘

calculate

计算

letter

字母

alphabet

字母表

word

字

text

课文

read

读

chalk

粉笔

lesson

上课

register

登记

exam

考试

certificate

证书

school uniform

校服

education

教育

encyclopedia

百科全书

university

大学

microscope

显微镜

map

地图

waste-paper basket

废纸篓

hotel
酒店

hostel
青年旅社

bureau de change
外币兑换处

car
汽车

language

语言

yes / no

是/否

Okay

好的

hello

您好

translator

翻译员

Thank you

谢谢

how much is...?

......多少钱？

I do not understand

我不明白

problem

问题

Good evening!

晚上好！

Good morning!

早上好！

Good night!

晚安！

bye bye

再见

direction

方向

luggage

行李

bag

包

backpack

双肩包

guest

客人

room

房间

sleeping bag

睡袋

tent

帐篷

tourist information

旅游信息

beach

海滩

credit card

信用卡

breakfast

早餐

lunch

午餐

dinner

晚餐

ticket

票

lift

电梯

stamp

邮票

border

边界

customs

海关

embassy

大使馆

visa

签证

passport

护照

travel - 旅行

aeroplane
飞机

ship
船

fire engine
消防车

bus
公交车

truck
卡车

motorboat
汽艇

bike
自行车

car
汽车

ferry

摆渡船

boat

小船

motorbike

摩托车

police car

警车

racing car

赛车

rental car

租车

car sharing

拼车

breakdown truck

拖车

refuse truck

垃圾车

motor

发动机

fuel

汽油

petrol station

加油站

traffic sign

交通标志

traffic

交通

traffic jam

交通堵塞

car park

停车场

train station

火车站

tracks

轨道

train

火车

tram

电车

carriage

货车

transport - 交通运输

helicopter

直升机

airport

机场

tower

塔

passenger

乘客

container

集装箱

carton

纸板箱

cart

手推车

basket

篮子

take off / land

起飞/降落

city

城市

village

村庄

city centre

市中心

house

房子

cinema
电影院

advert
广告

CINEMA

street lamp
路灯

street
街道

taxi
出租车

snack shop
小吃店

pedestrian
行人

pavement
人行道

zebra crossing
斑马线

bin
垃圾箱

crossing
十字路口

traffic lights
红绿灯

hut

小屋

flat

公寓

train station

火车站

town hall

市政厅

museum

博物馆

school

学校

university

大学

bank

银行

hospital

医院

hotel

酒店

pharmacy

药房

office

办公室

book shop

书店

shop

商店

florist's

花店

supermarket

超市

market

市场

department store

百货商店

fishmonger's

鱼店

shopping centre

购物中心

harbour

海港

city - 城市

park

公园

bench

长凳

bridge

桥

stairs

楼梯

underground

地铁

tunnel

隧道

bus stop

公交车站

bar

酒吧

restaurant

餐馆

postbox

邮筒

street sign

路标

parking meter

停车计时器

zoo

动物园

swimming pool

游泳馆

mosque

清真寺

farm
农场

pollution
污染

graveyard
墓地

church
教堂

playground
操场

temple
寺庙

landscape
地形

signpost 指示牌
way 路
meadow 草地
stone 石头
tree 树
hiker 徒步旅行者
river 河
grass 草
flower 花

valley

峡谷

hill

山

lake

湖

forest

森林

desert

沙漠

volcano

火山

castle

城堡

rainbow

彩虹

mushroom

蘑菇

palm tree

棕榈树

mosquito

蚊子

fly

苍蝇

ant

蚂蚁

bee

蜜蜂

spider

蜘蛛

beetle

甲虫

frog

青蛙

squirrel

松鼠

hedgehog

刺猬

hare

野兔

owl

猫头鹰

bird

鸟

swan

天鹅

boar

野猪

deer

鹿

moose

麋鹿

dam

水坝

wind turbine

风力发电机

solar panel

太阳能电池板

climate

气候

waiter
服务员

menu
菜单

chair
椅子

soup
汤

pizza
披萨饼

cutlery
餐具

tablecloth
桌布

starter
前菜

main course
主菜

dessert
甜点

drinks
饮料

food
食物

bottle
瓶子

fast food

快餐

street food

街边小吃

teapot

茶壶

sugar bowl

糖盒

portion

一份饭菜

espresso machine

意式咖啡机

high chair

高脚椅

bill

账单

tray

托盘

knife

刀

fork

餐叉

spoon

勺子

teaspoon

茶匙

serviette

餐巾

glass

玻璃杯

plate

碟子

soup plate

汤盘

saucer

碟子

sauce

酱

salt pot

盐瓶

pepper mill

胡椒磨

vinegar

醋

oil

食用油

spices

调味料

ketchup

番茄酱

mustard

芥末

mayonnaise

蛋黄酱

special offer
特价

customer
顾客

dairy
乳制品

fruit
水果

trolley
购物车

butcher's

肉铺

baker's

面包房

weigh

称重

vegetables

蔬菜

meat

肉

frozen food

冷冻食品

cold meat

冷盘

tinned food

罐头食品

washing powder

洗衣粉

sweets

甜食

household products

日用品

cleaning products

清洁用品

salesperson

销售员

till

收银机

cashier

收银员

shopping list

购物清单

opening hours

开放时间

wallet

钱包

credit card

信用卡

bag

袋子

plastic bag

塑料袋

water

水

juice

果汁

milk

牛奶

coke

可乐

wine

红酒

beer

啤酒

alcohol

酒

cocoa

可可

tea

茶

coffee

咖啡

espresso

意式浓缩咖啡

cappuccino

卡布奇诺

banana

香蕉

apple

苹果

orange

橙子

melon

西瓜

lemon

柠檬

carrot

胡萝卜

garlic

大蒜

bamboo

竹子

onion

洋葱

mushroom

蘑菇

nuts

坚果

noodles

面条

spaghetti

意大利面条

rice

米饭

salad

沙拉

chips

薯条

fried potatoes

炸土豆

pizza

披萨饼

hamburger

汉堡包

sandwich

三明治

cutlet

炸猪排

ham

火腿

salami

萨拉米

sausage

香肠

chicken

鸡肉

roast

烤肉

fish

鱼

porridge oats

燕麦片

muesli

穆兹利

cornflakes

玉米片

flour

面粉

croissant

羊角面包

bread roll

面包卷

bread

面包

toast

烤面包

biscuits

饼干

butter

黄油

curd

凝乳

cake

蛋糕

egg

蛋

fried egg

煎蛋

cheese

奶酪

ice cream

冰激凌

sugar

糖

honey

蜂蜜

jam

果酱

chocolate spread

巧克力酱

curry

咖喱饭

goat

山羊

cow

奶牛

calf

牛犊

pig

猪

piglet

小猪

bull

公牛

goose
鹅

duck
鸭

chick
小鸡

hen
母鸡

cock
公鸡

rat
鼠

cat
猫

mouse
老鼠

ox
牛

dog
狗

doghouse
狗屋

garden hose
花园浇水软管

watering can
洒水壶

scythe
长柄大镰刀

plough
犁

sickle

镰刀

hoe

锄头

pitchfork

长柄草耙

axe

斧头

wheelbarrow

独轮手推车

trough

饲料槽

milk can

牛奶罐

sack

麻布袋

fence

栅栏

stable

马厩

greenhouse

温室

soil

土壤

seed

种子

fertilizer

肥料

combine harvester

联合收割机

farm - 农场

harvest

收割

harvest

收割

yams

山药

wheat

小麦

soy

大豆

potato

土豆

corn

玉米

rapeseed

油菜籽

fruit tree

果树

cassava

树薯

cereals

谷物

farm - 农场

living room

客厅

bathroom

浴室

kitchen

厨房

bedroom

卧室

child's room

儿童房

dining room

餐厅

floor

地板

wall

墙壁

ceiling

吊顶

cellar

地窖

sauna

桑拿

balcony

阳台

terrace

露台

pool

游泳池

lawn mower

割草机

sheet

被单

bedspread

床罩

bed

床

broom

扫帚

bucket

水桶

switch

开关

carpet

地毯

curtain

窗帘

table

餐桌

chair

椅子

rocking chair

摇椅

armchair

扶手椅

book

书

blanket

毯子

decoration

装饰品

firewood

木柴

film

电影

hi-fi equipment

高保真音响

key

钥匙

newspaper

报纸

painting

油画

poster

海报

radio

收音机

notepad

笔记本

hoover

吸尘器

cactus

仙人掌

candle

蜡烛

fridge
冰箱

microwave oven
微波炉

kitchen scales
厨房秤

detergent
洗洁精

toaster
烤面包机

oven
烤箱

freezer
冰柜

dishwasher
洗碗机

cooker

炊具

pot

锅

cast-iron pot

铸铁锅

wok / kadai

炒锅

pan

平底锅

kettle

水壶

steamer

蒸锅

baking tray

烤盘

crockery

陶瓷锅

mug

马克杯

bowl

碗

chopsticks

筷子

ladle

长柄勺

spatula

铲子

whisk

搅拌器

strainer

滤网

sieve

筛子

grater

磨碎机

mortar

研钵

barbecue

烧烤

open fire

明火

chopping board

菜板

rolling pin

擀面杖

corkscrew

开瓶器

can

罐子

can opener

开罐器

pot holder

隔热手套

sink

水槽

brush

刷子

sponge

海绵

blender

搅拌机

deep freezer

冷藏箱

baby bottle

奶瓶

tap

水龙头

heating
供暖设备

shower
淋浴

towel
毛巾

shower curtain
浴帘

bubble bath
泡沫浴

bathtub
浴缸

glass
玻璃杯

washing machine
洗衣机

tiles
瓷砖

tap
水龙头

potty
便壶

sink
水槽

toilet
厕所

squat toilet
蹲便器

bidet
坐浴器

urinal
小便池

toilet paper
厕纸

toilet brush
马桶刷

toothbrush

牙刷

toothpaste

牙膏

dental floss

牙线

wash

洗

handheld shower

手持式喷淋头

douche

冲洗器

basin

洗脸盆

back brush

擦背刷

soap

肥皂

shower gel

沐浴露

shampoo

洗发水

flannel

法兰绒

drain

排水

cream

乳霜

deodorant

除臭剂

mirror

镜子

hand mirror

手镜

razor

剃须刀

shaving foam

剃须泡沫

aftershave

须后水

comb

梳子

brush

刷子

hair dryer

吹风机

hairspray

喷发定型剂

makeup

化妆品

lipstick

唇膏

nail varnish

指甲油

cotton wool

化妆棉

nail scissors

指甲剪

perfume

香水

washbag

洗漱包

stool

凳子

weighing scale

计重秤

bathrobe

浴袍

rubber gloves

橡胶手套

tampon

卫生棉条

sanitary towel

卫生巾

chemical toilet

化学厕所

alarm clock
闹钟

cuddly toy
毛绒玩具

toy car
玩具车

rattle
拨浪鼓

doll's house
玩具屋

present
礼物

balloon

气球

bed

床

pram

（洋娃娃用）婴儿车

deck of cards

扑克牌

jigsaw

拼图

comic

漫画

lego bricks

乐高积木

building blocks

积木玩具

action figure

玩具人

babygrow

婴儿服

frisbee

飞盘

mobile

床铃玩具

board game

棋盘游戏

dice

骰子

model train set

火车模型

dummy

安抚奶嘴

party

聚会

picture book

绘本

ball

球

doll

洋娃娃

play

玩

sandpit

沙坑

swing

秋千

toys

玩具

video game console

游戏机

tricycle

三轮车

teddy bear

泰迪熊

wardrobe

衣柜

clothing

衣服

socks

袜子

stockings

长袜

tights

紧身裤

scarf
围巾

umbrella
雨伞

t-shirt
T恤

belt
皮带

boots
靴子

slippers
拖鞋

trainers
运动鞋

sandals
凉鞋

shoes
鞋

rubber boots
雨靴

underpants
内裤

bra
胸罩

vest
背心

clothing - 衣服

45

body

身体

trousers

裤子

jeans

牛仔裤

skirt

短裙

blouse

女式衬衫

shirt

衬衫

pullover

套头衫

hoodie

卫衣

blazer

西装夹克

jacket

夹克

coat

外套

raincoat

雨衣

costume

套装

dress

连衣裙

wedding dress

婚纱

suit

西装

nightgown

睡袍

pyjamas

睡衣

sari

莎丽

headscarf

头巾

turban

包头巾

burqa

波卡

kaftan

卡夫坦

abaya

(阿拉伯式)长袍长袍

swimsuit

泳衣

trunks

男式泳裤

shorts

短裤

tracksuit

运动服

apron

围裙

gloves

手套

button

纽扣

glasses

眼镜

bracelet

手链

necklace

项链

ring

戒指

earring

耳环

cap

便帽

coat hanger

衣架

hat

帽子

tie

领带

zip

拉链

helmet

头盔

braces

背带

school uniform

校服

uniform

制服

bib
围兜

dummy
安抚奶嘴

nappy
尿不湿

server
服务器

filing cabinet
文件柜

printer
打印机

monitor
显示屏

paper
纸

mouse
鼠标

desk
办公桌

folder
文件夹

keyboard
键盘

waste-paper basket
废纸筐

chair
椅子

computer
电脑

coffee mug
咖啡杯

calculator
计算器

internet
因特网

laptop

笔记本电脑

letter

信件

message

消息

mobile

手机

network

网络

photocopier

复印机

software

软件

telephone

电话

plug socket

插座

fax machine

传真机

form

表格

document

文件

buy

买

pay

付钱

trade

交易

money

现金

dollar

美元

euro

欧元

yen

日元

rouble

卢布

Swiss franc

瑞士法郎

renminbi yuan

人民币

rupee

卢比

cashpoint

提款处

bureau de change

外币兑换处

gold

金

silver

银

oil

石油

energy

能源

price

价格

contract

合同

tax

税金

stock

股票

work

工作

employee

职员

employer

老板

factory

工厂

shop

商店

police officer
警官

fireman
消防员

pilot
飞行员

doctor
医生

cook
厨师

gardener
- - - - - - - -
园丁

carpenter
- - - - - - - -
木匠

seamstress
- - - - - - - -
裁缝

judge
- - - - - - - -
法官

chemist
- - - - - - - -
化学家

actor
- - - - - - - -
演员

bus driver

公交车司机

taxi driver

出租车司机

fisherman

渔夫

cleaning lady

清洁女工

roofer

屋顶工

waiter

服务员

hunter

猎人

painter

画家

baker

面包师

electrician

电工

builder

建筑工人

engineer

工程师

butcher

屠夫

plumber

水管工

postman

邮递员

soldier

士兵

architect

建筑师

cashier

收银员

florist

花农

hairdresser

理发师

conductor

售票员

mechanic

机械师

captain

船长

dentist

牙医

scientist

科学家

rabbi

拉比

imam

伊玛目

monk

和尚

clergyman

牧师

hammer
铁锤

screwdriver
螺丝刀

pliers
钳子

spanner
扳手

torch
手电筒

digger
挖掘机

toolbox
工具箱

ladder
梯子

saw
锯子

nails
钉子

drill
钻机

repair

修

shovel

铲子

Damn!

靠！

dustpan

簸箕

paint pot

油漆桶

screws

螺丝

musical instruments

乐器

drum kit
打击乐器

loudspeaker
扬声器

guitar
吉他

double bass
低音提琴

trumpet
小号

piano

钢琴

violin

小提琴

bass

贝斯

timpani

定音鼓

drums

鼓

keyboard

电子琴

saxophone

萨克斯管

flute

长笛

microphone

麦克风

entrance
入口

tiger
老虎

cage
笼子

zebra
斑马

animal feed
动物饲料

panda
熊猫

animals

动物

elephant

大象

kangaroo

袋鼠

rhino

犀牛

gorilla

大猩猩

bear

熊

camel

骆驼

ostrich

鸵鸟

lion

狮子

monkey

猴子

flamingo

火烈鸟

parrot

鹦鹉

polar bear

北极熊

penguin

企鹅

shark

鲨鱼

peacock

孔雀

snake

蛇

crocodile

鳄鱼

zookeeper

动物园管理员

seal

海豹

jaguar

美洲豹

pony

矮种马

leopard

豹

hippo

河马

giraffe

长颈鹿

eagle

老鹰

boar

野猪

fish

鱼

turtle

龟

walrus

海象

fox

狐狸

gazelle

羚羊

American football
橄榄球

cycling
骑自行车

tennis
网球

basketball
篮球

swimming
游泳

boxing
拳击

ice hockey
冰球

football
英式足球

badminton
羽毛球

athletics
田径

handball
手球

skiing
滑雪

polo
马球

jump
跳

laugh
笑

hug
拥抱

walk
走路

sing
唱

dream
做梦

pray
祈祷

kiss
亲吻

write
书写

draw
画

show
展示

push
推

give
给

take
拿

have
有

do
做

be
当

stand
站

run
跑

pull
拉

throw
扔

fall
摔倒

lie
躺

wait
等待

carry
携带

sit
坐

get dressed
穿衣

sleep
睡觉

wake up
醒来

look at
看

cry
哭

stroke
抚摸

comb
梳头

talk
交谈

understand
明白

ask
问

listen
听

drink
喝

eat
吃

tidy up
清理

love
爱

cook
做饭

drive
开车

fly
飞

sail

航行

calculate

计算

read

读

learn

学习

work

工作

marry

结婚

sew

缝

brush teeth

刷牙

kill

杀

smoke

抽烟

send

寄

grandmother
祖母

grandfather
祖父

father
父亲

mother
母亲

baby
婴童

daughter
女儿

son
儿子

guest
客人

aunt
阿姨

uncle
叔叔

brother
兄弟

sister
姐妹

body

身体

forehead
前额

eye
眼睛

shoulder
肩膀

finger
手指

face
脸

chin
下巴

hand
手

breast
乳房

leg
腿

arm
手臂

baby

婴童

man

男人

woman

女人

girl

女孩

boy

男孩

head

头

body - 身体

back

背部

belly

肚子

belly button

肚脐

toe

脚趾

heel

脚后跟

bone

骨头

hip

臀部

knee

膝盖

elbow

手肘

nose

鼻子

bottom

屁股

skin

皮肤

cheek

脸颊

ear

耳朵

lip

嘴唇

body - 身体

mouth

嘴

tooth

牙齿

tongue

舌头

brain

脑

heart

心脏

muscle

肌肉

lung

肺

liver

肝脏

stomach

胃

kidneys

肾脏

sex

性交

condom

避孕套

ovum

卵子

semen

精子

pregnancy

怀孕

body - 身体

menstruation

月经

vagina

阴道

penis

阴茎

eyebrow

眉毛

hair

头发

neck

脖子

hospital

医院

hospital
医院

ambulance
救护车

wheelchair
轮椅

fracture
骨折

doctor

医生

emergency room

急诊室

nurse

护士

emergency

紧急情况

unconscious

昏迷

pain

痛

injury

受伤

bleeding

出血

heart attack

心脏病发作

stroke

中风

allergy

过敏

cough

咳嗽

fever

发烧

flu

流感

diarrhoea

腹泻

headache

头痛

cancer

癌症

diabetes

糖尿病

surgeon

外科医生

scalpel

手术刀

operation

手术

hospital - 医院

CT

CT

x-ray

X光

ultrasound

超声波

face mask

口罩

disease

疾病

waiting room

候诊室

crutch

拐杖

plaster

石膏

bandage

绷带

injection

注射

stethoscope

听诊器

stretcher

担架

clinical thermometer

体温计

birth

出生

overweight

超重

hearing aid

助听器

disinfectant

消毒液

infection

感染

virus

病毒

HIV / AIDS

艾滋病

medicine

药物

vaccination

接种疫苗

tablets

药片

pill

药丸

emergency call

急救电话

blood pressure monitor

血压计

ill / healthy

生病/健康

Help!
救命！

alarm
警报

assault
突击

attack
攻击

danger
危险

emergency exit
紧急出口

Fire!
着火啦！

fire extinguisher
灭火器

accident
意外

first-aid kit
急救箱

SOS
呼救信号

police
警察

Europe

欧洲

North America

北美洲

South America

南美洲

Africa

非洲

Asia

亚洲

Australia

澳洲

Atlantic

大西洋

Pacific

太平洋

Indian Ocean

印度洋

Antarctic Ocean

南冰洋

Arctic Ocean

北冰洋

North Pole

北极

South Pole
南极

Antarctica
南极洲

Earth
地球

land
陆地

sea
海

island
岛

nation
国家

state
国家

clock face

钟面

hour hand

时针

minute hand

分针

second hand

秒针

What time is it?

现在几点？

day

天

time

时间

now

现在

digital watch

电子表

minute

分

hour

时

Monday
周一

Wednesday
周三

Friday
周五

Tuesday
周二

Saturday
周六

Thursday
周四

Sunday
周日

yesterday

昨天

today

今天

tomorrow

明天

morning

早晨

noon

中午

evening

晚上

business days

工作日

weekend

周末

rain
雨

snow
雪

wind
风

spring
春

autumn
秋

summer
夏

winter
冬

weather forecast

天气预报

thermometer

温度计

sunshine

阳光

cloud

云

fog

雾

humidity

潮湿

lightning

闪电

thunder

打雷

storm

风暴

hail

冰雹

monsoon

季风

flood

洪水

ice

冰

January

一月

February

二月

March

三月

April

四月

May

五月

June

六月

July

七月

August

八月

September

九月

October

十月

November

十一月

December

十二月

circle

圆形

square

正方形

rectangle

长方形

triangle

三角形

sphere

球体

cube

立方体

white

白

yellow

黄

orange

橙

pink

粉

red

红

purple

紫

blue

蓝

green

绿

brown

棕

grey

灰

black

黑

a lot / a little

很多/少许

angry / calm

生气/平静

beautiful / ugly

美/丑

beginning / end

首/尾

big / small

大/小

bright / dark

明/暗

brother / sister

兄弟/姐妹

clean / dirty

干净/肮脏

complete / incomplete

完整/缺失

day / night

白天/晚上

dead / alive

死/生

wide / narrow

宽/窄

edible / inedible

可食用/非食用

evil / kind

邪恶/善良

excited / bored

兴奋/无聊

fat / thin

胖/瘦

first / last

第一/最后

friend / enemy

朋友/敌人

full / empty

满/空

hard / soft

硬/软

heavy / light

重/轻

hunger / thirst

饿/渴

ill / healthy

生病/健康

illegal / legal

非法/合法

intelligent / stupid

聪明/愚笨

left / right

左/右

near / far

近/远

opposites - 反义词

new / used

新/旧

nothing / something

没有/有些

old / young

老/幼

on / off

开/关

open / closed

打开/合上

quiet / loud

安静/吵闹

rich / poor

富/穷

right / wrong

对/错

rough / smooth

粗糙/光滑

sad / happy

伤心/高兴

short / long

短/长

slow / fast

慢/快

wet / dry

湿/干

warm / cool

温暖/凉爽

war / peace

战争/和平

0

zero

零

1

one

一

2

two

二

3

three

三

4

four

四

5

five

五

6

six

六

7

seven

七

8

eight

八

9

nine

九

10

ten

十

11

eleven

十一

12

twelve

十二

13

thirteen

十三

14

fourteen

十四

15

fifteen

十五

16

sixteen

十六

17

seventeen

十七

18

eighteen

十八

19

nineteen

十九

20

twenty

二十

100

hundred

百

1.000

thousand

千

1.000.000

million

百万

languages

语言

English

英语

American English

美式英语

Chinese Mandarin

普通话

Hindi

印地语

Spanish

西班牙语

French

法语

Arabic

阿拉伯语

Russian

俄语

Portuguese

葡萄牙语

Bengali

孟加拉语

German

德语

Japanese

日语

I

我

you

你

he / she / it

他/她/它

we

我们

you

你们

they

他们

who?

谁？

what?

什么？

how?

怎样？

where?

哪里？

when?

什么时候？

name

名字

behind

后面

in

里面

in front of

前面

over

上方

on

上面

under

下面

beside

旁边

between

中间

place

地点